WHAT IS CRYPTO AIRDROP?

"Maximizing Your Earnings with Airdrop: A Step-by-Step Guide"

BY

DARLINGTON NWEKE

December, 2022.

TABLE OF CONTENT

INTRODUCTION

Crypto Airdrops are a relatively new way of distributing digital assets to a large group of individuals, typically for free. It is becoming an increasingly popular method of introducing new tokens and coins to the crypto space. A crypto airdrop is a marketing strategy in which a blockchain project distributes tokens or coins to the crypto community. It is a way for projects to gain exposure, build a larger user base, and reward early adopters. Airdrops are usually distributed to an existing base of users who hold a certain cryptocurrency, such as Bitcoin or Ethereum. In some cases, the airdrop may require that users complete certain tasks, such as following a Twitter account, subscribing to a newsletter, or joining a Telegram group.

Crypto airdrops are becoming increasingly popular as a way for crypto projects to gain exposure, reward existing users, and create a larger user base. Crypto airdrops can also be used to stimulate the market and increase liquidity. Airdrops are a great way to get involved in the crypto world and get free coins or tokens. They can be a great way to learn more about the project and potentially make some money in the process.

If you are interested in getting involved in crypto airdrops, it is important to do your research. Make sure you understand the project and its goals, as well as any requirements for participation. Additionally, be sure to stay up to date on the latest news and announcements, as airdrops can change quickly.

Overall, crypto airdrops are a great way to get involved in the crypto world and potentially make some money in the process. With the right research and understanding, you can benefit from participating in crypto a

CHAPTER 1

WHAT IS A CRYPTO AIRDROP?

Airdrops are essentially free giveaways of tokens or coins, usually as a form of marketing, to increase awareness and usage of a particular cryptocurrency. Airdrops are becoming increasingly popular as a way for cryptocurrency projects to get their tokens into the hands of users, who can then trade them, use them, or simply hold onto them as an investment. With a crypto airdrop, users can get free tokens just for participating in a simple activity, such as following a project on social media, or referring a friend. Airdrops can be a great way to get your hands on some free tokens, so if you're interested in trying out a new cryptocurrency project, make sure to look out for upcoming airdrops and join in!

Crypto airdrop is a type of crypto giveaway where a blockchain project distributes free tokens or coins to the crypto community. This is usually done to create a user base and generate buzz about a project. Crypto Airdrops are a great way to get free cryptocurrency tokens without having to spend any money.

Airdrops allow blockchain projects to give away a portion of their tokens to the public. This is usually done to promote the project and increase awareness, often in exchange for simple tasks like joining a Telegram group, retweeting a tweet, or signing up for a newsletter.

A crypto airdrop is a promotional activity that involves distributing free tokens or coins to a large number of cryptocurrency wallet addresses. Crypto airdrops are primarily done to increase the awareness of a project, incentivize participation, and to reward existing holders of related tokens.

An airdrop is similar to a traditional product or service giveaway in that it is a promotional technique used to attract new users and drive adoption. The difference is that, instead of awarding physical goods, airdrops reward users with digital assets, such as tokens or coins.

Airdrops can be structured in a variety of ways, such as giving away a certain amount of tokens to each address, or distributing tokens according to a predetermined formula, such as airdropping tokens to every 100th address. Recipients can often claim their tokens by submitting a form, joining a telegram channel, or joining the project's social media accounts.

Crypto airdrops are beneficial to both the project owners and the users. For project owners, airdrops can be an effective way to increase the awareness of their project and its tokens. For users, airdrops can be a great way to get free tokens and potentially benefit from the appreciation of the token's value over time.

However, it is important for users to remember that there are potential risks associated with participating in airdrops. These risks include the possibility of scams, as well as the risk of accidental token loss. It is therefore important to do your own research and understand the project before participating in an airdrop.

generally, crypto airdrops are an effective way for project owners to promote their projects and reward users, while offering users the chance to potentially benefit from the appreciation of token values. However, it is important to remember that there are risks associated with

participating in airdrops, so be sure to do your own research before participating.

BENEFITS OF PARTICIPATING IN AN AIRDROP

1. Airdrops are a great way to promote a project or a cryptocurrency: Airdrops are an effective way to promote a cryptocurrency project. Airdrops are a form of marketing, where free tokens or coins are given to a large number of wallet addresses to spread awareness of the project. Airdrops are also a great way to incentivize and reward early adopters of a project. By distributing free tokens, people are more likely to be interested in the project and may even purchase more tokens or coins to support the project. Airdrops can also bring more liquidity to a project's token, making it easier to trade and potentially increasing its price.

Furthermore, airdrops can help a project increase its visibility and build a larger community of users. By distributing tokens to people who may not even know what a cryptocurrency is, a project can potentially bring in new users that were not previously aware of the project. This can lead to more adoption and usage of the project, which can result in more value for the cryptocurrency.

generally, airdrops are an effective way to promote a cryptocurrency project and can help to increase visibility and usage.

2. Airdrops can help create a large and engaged community for a project or coin: Airdropping is a great way to create a large community for engagement on a cryptocurrency project. By airdropping coins or tokens to a large group of users, it creates a sense of ownership and encourages the users to engage with the project. Users may be incentivized to hold the coins or tokens, use them to purchase goods and services, or trade them on exchanges. Additionally, users

may be motivated to spread the word about the project and encourage others to join, helping to build and expand the community.

By providing users with free coins or tokens, airdrops can also increase visibility and popularity. This can be a great way to introduce a new project to the crypto community, and it provides the project with a ready-made user base to draw from. Airdrops can also be used to reward existing users of the project, which helps to create loyalty and encourages further engagement. This can be a great way to ensure that the project continues to grow, and that the community remains active and engaged.

3. Airdrops can help increase brand awareness and reach new markets: Airdrop is a great way to create brand awareness because it allows you to send your brand's message to a wide-reaching audience quickly and efficiently. It allows you to promote your brand to those who are already interested in your services, as well as to those who may not have heard of your brand before. Airdrop is a great tool for creating awareness and increasing engagement with potential customers. Additionally, it can be used to reward loyal customers with incentives, such as discounts and free products, helping to increase customer loyalty and brand recognition.

Overall, airdrop is an effective tool to use in order to create brand awareness and increase customer engagement.

4. Airdrops are an easy way to earn free crypto coins: Airdrops are a great way to get free crypto coins. When a company holds an airdrop, they distribute a limited amount of coins to people who fit their criteria. This is usually based on following the project on social media or holding a certain amount

of coins. Airdrops are a great way to get free coins and increase your holdings. They can also be a great way to learn about new projects and get involved in the crypto community.

The main benefit of airdrops is that it allows you to get free coins without having to pay for them. This means that you can increase your holdings without having to spend money. It also allows you to get acquainted with new projects and potentially make some money if the project is successful. Airdrops are a great way to get free crypto coins and increase your holdings.

However, there are some potential risks associated with airdrops. Airdrops can be scams, as some companies may be looking to take advantage of people. Additionally, some airdrops may require personal information in order to participate. It is important to research the project carefully before participating in an airdrop.

5. Airdrops can be an effective way to increase liquidity for a cryptocurrency: Airdrop is a promotional strategy for cryptocurrency coins whereby coins or tokens are distributed for free to a large number of wallet addresses which in turn increases the coin's liquidity, as the airdropped coins are available to be traded on exchanges. Additionally, airdrops help to increase the number of users who own and use the coins, and thus can help with the long-term success and acceptance of the coin.

By giving away free coins, those who receive the coins may feel more inclined to hold onto the coins long-term instead of immediately selling them, which helps to increase the liquidity of the coin. Airdrops are also used to attract new users to the coin, as it is a free and easy way for people to get started with the coin. By increasing the user base, the coin can become more widely accepted and thus have more liquidity.

6. Participating in an airdrop can help to build a portfolio of diverse cryptocurrencies: Participating in an airdrop can help build a portfolio of diverse cryptocurrencies by providing an opportunity to receive free tokens from different blockchain projects. Airdrops can help diversify a portfolio and provide exposure to a variety of projects that may have otherwise gone unnoticed or not been accessible to the individual. Airdrops also allow individuals to gain early access to tokens that could potentially increase in value over time. By participating in airdrops, individuals can increase their portfolio's diversification and potentially increase their returns on investments.

Airdrops are also a great way to learn more about different blockchain projects and the cryptocurrencies associated with them. By researching the airdrops, participants can gain an understanding of the technology and the project's goals. This knowledge can be used to make educated decisions on whether or not to invest in these projects in the future.

Overall, participating in an airdrop can be an effective way to build a portfolio of diverse cryptocurrencies. It can provide exposure to a variety of projects, offer potential returns, and teach individuals more about the crypto space

CHAPTER 2

HOW TO PARTICIPATE IN CRYPTOCURRENCY AIRDROPS

There are 3 simple summarized ways of participating in an airdrop project, these are:

A. Finding Crypto Airdrops: to find an eligible crypto airdrop projects, follow the following guides:

1. Follow crypto-related social media accounts: One of the best ways to stay up to date on crypto airdrops is to follow crypto-related social media accounts, such as Twitter, Reddit, and Telegram. Companies often post updates about upcoming airdrops, as well as other interesting news related to the industry.

2. Join crypto-related discussion groups: A great way to get the latest news on crypto airdrops is to join crypto-related discussion groups. These groups often discuss the latest happenings in the crypto world, and are a great way to stay informed about upcoming airdrops.

3. Check crypto-related websites: There are several crypto-focused websites that regularly post updates about upcoming

crypto airdrops, for example, CoinMarketCap and CryptoCompare. These websites also often provide additional tips and advice on how to participate in airdrops.

4. Monitor crypto forums: Crypto forums are a great way to get the latest news on upcoming airdrops. Many of these forums such as reddit and BitcoinTalk also provide additional information on the airdrop, such as the requirements for participation, the time frame for the airdrop, and what type of currency will be distributed.

5. Subscribe to crypto-related newsletters: Many crypto-related websites and newsletters offer subscriptions that will alert you when new airdrops are available. Subscribing to one of these newsletters can be a great way to stay up to date on the latest airdrops.

6. Follow crypto influencers: Crypto influencers such as Vitalik Buterin and Andreas Antonopoulos often tweet about upcoming airdrops. Following them on Twitter can help you stay on top of the latest news.

B. Signing Up for Crypto Airdrops: Signing up for a crypto airdrop is a great way to get involved in the world of cryptocurrency. Airdrops are a great way to get free tokens or coins that can be traded on exchanges for other cryptocurrencies. To get started, you'll need to find a reputable airdrop that is offering the tokens you want. After that, you'll need to complete the registration process and provide any necessary information. Once you're registered, you may need to complete a few tasks such as following them on social media, or referring others to join the airdrop. Once all the tasks are completed, you'll receive the tokens you signed up for. One thing to note is that not all airdrops are legitimate, so make sure to do your due diligence before signing up.

C. Establishing an Eligible Wallet: Creating an eligible wallet for participating in a crypto airdrop typically involves downloading a wallet that is compatible with the currency being airdropped. Once the wallet is downloaded, the user should follow the instructions given by the airdrop issuer to claim the airdrop tokens. This can involve submitting their wallet address or performing additional tasks such as liking and sharing social media posts. Additionally, the user should make sure to read any terms and conditions related to the airdrop to ensure they are eligible to receive the tokens.

Once the user has completed the steps required to claim the airdrop, they should ensure that their wallet address is correct and that they have securely backed up their wallet. They should also keep their wallet secure and up-to-date to ensure that they are able to access their tokens after the airdrop has ended.

THINGS TO CONSIDER WHEN PARTICIPATING IN A CRYPTO AIRDROP

1. Check the legitimacy of the airdrop: Not all airdrops are legitimate, and some may be scams. Do your research and make sure the airdrop is real before participating.

2. Understand the terms and conditions: Make sure you understand the terms and conditions of the airdrop before participating. Know what is expected of you and what you can expect in return.

3. Make sure you have enough space: Airdrops can require you to have a certain amount of space in your wallet for the tokens, so make sure you have enough space before participating.

4. Have the correct wallet address: Make sure you have the correct wallet address for the airdrop. If you have the wrong address, your tokens may be lost forever.

5. Keep your private keys secure: Make sure you keep your private keys secure and never share them with anyone.

6. Be patient: Airdrops can take some time to be distributed, so be patient and don't expect your tokens right away.

CHAPTER 3

HOW TO MAKE MONEY WITH AIRDROPS

Airdrops are one of the newest ways to make money online. Airdrops involve companies or projects giving away free tokens or coins in exchange for promotional activities such as sharing a link or posting on social media. The idea is to reward people for their support and to spread the word about a particular project.

To make money with Airdrops, first you have to find a good project to join. Research the project's background, its team and its roadmap. You can find airdrops listed on websites such as Airdropalert.com and Airdrops.io.

Once you have chosen a project, you will need to register for the airdrop and complete the steps required. These can include joining a Telegram group, liking a Facebook page or even tweeting about the project. You will then be rewarded with tokens or coins for your efforts.

When you receive your tokens or coins, you will need to store them in a secure cryptocurrency wallet. This will help protect your tokens or coins and will make them easier to transfer.

You can make money with Airdrops by holding onto the tokens or coins and waiting for them to appreciate in value. However, this is not a surefire way to make money, as the value of the tokens or coins can go down as well as up.

You can also make money with airdrops by trading the tokens or coins on exchanges. Make sure to do your research and keep an eye on the market before engaging in any trades.

Airdrops can be an easy and effective way to make money online. With the right research and effort, you can gain some extra income from airdrops.

Good luck!

TIPS FOR MAKING THE MOST OF CRYPTO AIRDROPS

1. Follow Cryptocurrency Accounts on Social Media: Staying up to date on cryptocurrency news and announcements is key to making the most of crypto airdrops. Following cryptocurrency accounts on social media can help you stay informed on upcoming airdrops, as well as other important news and updates.

2. Join Crypto Airdrop Alert Services: There are many airdrop alert services available that can help you stay informed on upcoming airdrops. Joining these services can help you stay ahead of the competition and make sure you don't miss out on any valuable airdrops.

3. Check Airdrop Requirements: Before signing up for an airdrop, make sure to read the requirements closely and make sure you meet them. Some airdrops may require you to have a certain amount of a specific cryptocurrency, or to have a certain number of followers on social media.

4. Join Airdrop Telegram & Discord Groups: Many cryptocurrency projects have active Telegram and Discord groups that you can join to stay informed on upcoming airdrops. Joining these groups can also give you the opportunity to ask questions and get advice from experienced airdrop hunters.

5. Claim Airdrops Quickly: Crypto airdrops are usually limited in number and are only available for a limited amount of time. It's important to claim airdrops quickly to make sure you don't miss out.

6. Monitor Your Airdrop Tokens: Once you've claimed airdrop tokens, make sure to monitor them closely. Some airdrops offer additional tokens if you hold the tokens for a certain amount of time or complete certain tasks.

7. Be Careful of Scams: Unfortunately, there are many scammers out there who are looking to take advantage of unsuspecting airdrop hunters. Always make sure to do your research and only sign up for airdrops from reputable sources.

CONCLUSION

Making money with crypto airdrop can be a great way to get involved in the cryptocurrency space without any upfront costs. It can also be a great way to get ahold of some free crypto, which can then be used to trade or invest in other cryptos. However, it is important to remember that crypto airdrops are typically high risk and sometimes can be scams, so it is important to do your research and ensure that you are getting involved in legitimate airdrops.

Additionally, it is important to remember that making money with crypto airdrop can be highly volatile and you should never invest money you cannot afford to lose.

Overall, crypto airdrops can be a great way to get involved in the cryptocurrency space and potentially make some money. A crypto airdrop is an effective and easy way to make money with cryptocurrency. It requires minimal effort, and you can potentially make a great return on your investments. With the right know-how and research, you can make money from these airdrops with relative ease. Take your time to get familiar with the process, research the projects offering airdrops, and stay informed of the latest trends. With a bit of luck and dedication, you could be well on your way to making money with crypto airdrops.

www.ingramcontent.com/pod-product-compliance
Lightning Source LLC
LaVergne TN
LVHW010508160826
845677LV00012B/2732

* 9 7 9 8 3 7 2 9 3 5 3 7 2 *